Play by the Rules

by Mary Butenhoff

Table of Contents

I need to know these words.

games

race

rules

runner

score

team

3

What Are Rules?

Do you know how to play games? All games have rules. You must learn the rules.

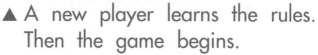
▲ A new player learns the rules. Then the game begins.

A rule tells what a player can do.
A rule tells what a player cannot do.

▲ The players can move the pieces
in different directions.

How Do Rules Help You Play a Game?

How does a game start? Some rules help players start a game.

▲ The referee throws a coin. The soccer game can start.

Each team must have the same number of players. Then the game will be fair.

▲ The rules tell how many players will play.

The game starts! How do you play the game? You have to know the rules.

▲ The players must listen to the referee.

A game is fun when you score a point. How do you count points? You have to know the rules.

▲ A player kicks the ball. He tries to score a point.

Do you like running in a race?
A runner must follow the rules.

▲ The runners must start at the same place.

A runner tries to run fast. The winner is the fastest in a race.

▲ This woman wins the race.

Why Are Rules Important?

A game must be fair. The rules help a game be fair.

 ▲ Everyone gets a turn in this game.

Some rules help a player be safe.
These players wear special shoes.

▲ These special shoes help keep players safe.

Some rules show a player how to be friendly. Some rules show players how to help each other.

▲ These players help each other.

All players must follow the rules.
Then all players have fun.

▲ Everyone plays by the rules.
Everyone has fun.

The rules make games fair.
The rules make games safe.
Then everyone has fun!